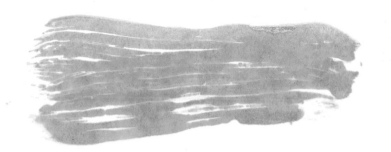

A CARIBBEAN COUNTING BOOK

compiled by Faustin Charles
illustrated by Roberta Arenson

BAREFOOT BOOKS
BATH

Introduction

It has always been easy for Caribbean children to make up rhymes. Caribbean speech is full of music and rhythm, and the hot tropical weather all year round gives the children the opportunity to play outdoors all the time. The children create games, songs and rhymes using the sounds and colours of the sea; the taste and variety of the fruits; the growth and flowering of trees and flowers; and the behaviour of insects, animals and people.

I collected these rhymes by visiting the Caribbean Islands and speaking to old people and to children at home and in school playgrounds. Some of the rhymes are old, some are new. They are all chanted as songs and in games.

When they are learning to count at school, especially in the rural villages, the children do so in a singing fashion. In this way, they remember their numbers quite easily, and also enjoy learning them. There are similarities to European and African counting rhymes, because the people of the Caribbean are descendants of people from these continents.

In translating counting rhymes from the Spanish, Dutch, and French-speaking territories, I have kept to the original text and rhythm of the languages. New dialects have sprung from speakers in these regions which reflect the music, humour, sadness and joy of everyday life.

Faustin Charles

One, two,
I makin' calaloo-stew!
Three, four,
Don't peep by de kitchen door!
Five, six,
Don't give me no tricks!
Seven, eight,
Why yuh can't wait!
Nine, ten,
Chile, I go tell yuh when!

Bahamas

One, two, three,
Mother catch a flea,
Flea die,
Mother cry,
One, two, three.
Four, five, six,
Mother get some sticks
They was long,
But not very strong,

Four, five, six.
Seven, eight, nine,
Mother get some twine
An' make a fishin' line;
Fish bite de line,
De stick break in half
An' de fish bust out a laugh!

Barbados

Mosquito one,
Mosquito two,
Mosquito jump in de ole man shoe;
De ole man cry,
De ole man cry,
De ole man cry like a little chile.
Mosquito three,
Mosquito four,
Mosquito light on a big pawpaw;
De pawpaw swell,
De pawpaw burst,
But it didn't stop de mosquito thirst.

Mosquito five,
Mosquito six,
Mosquito jump up on some bricks;
De bricks fall down,
De bricks fall down,
An' pin mosquito to de groun'.
Mosquito seven,
Mosquito eight,
Mosquito now full of fiery hate.
Mosquito nine,
Mosquito ten,
Mosquito bite two fat ole men.

Trinidad

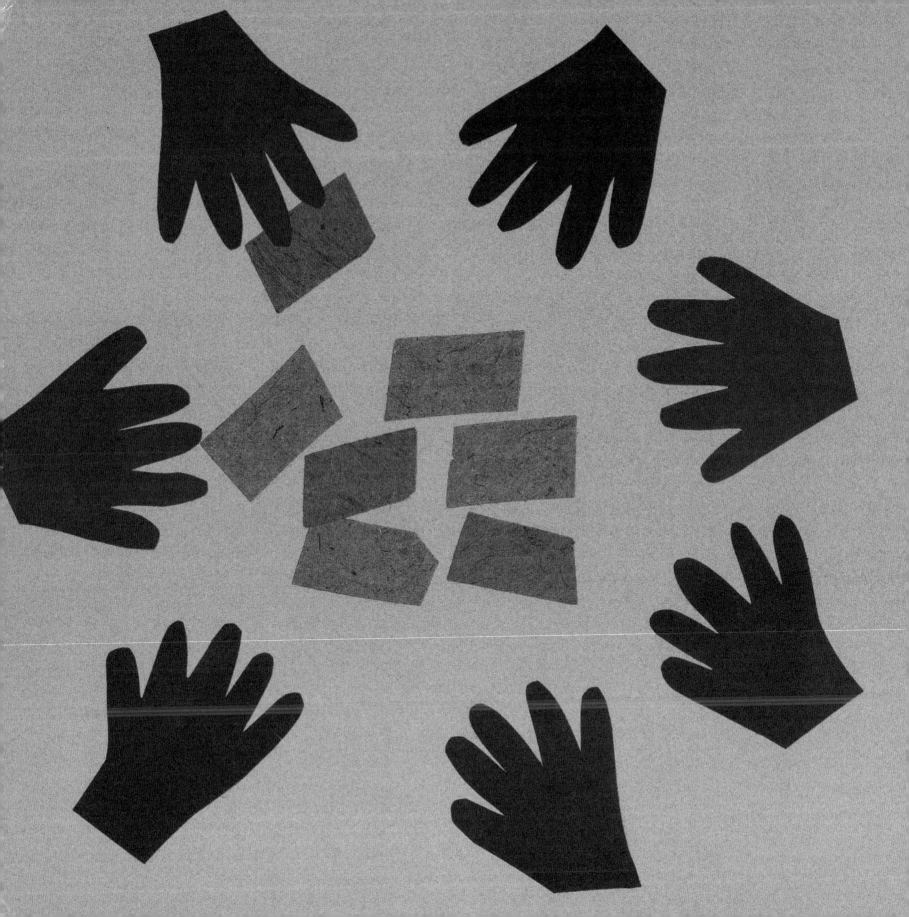

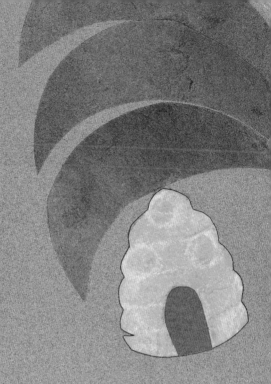

Seven little boys playin' wid wooden bricks,
One run away,
An' den there were six.
Six little boys playin' near a hive,
A bee stung one o' dem,
An' den there was five.
Five little boys playin' on de sea-shore,
A wave splash over one,
An' den there were four,
Four little boys peltin' stones in a tree,
A stone knocked out one,
An' den there were three.
Three little boys eatin' a stew,
One choke heself,
An' den there were two.
Two little boys havin' lotta fun,
One went an' lose heself,
An' den there was one.

Cuba

Ten little green bananas hangin' on a line,
A bird eat one,
Dat left nine.
Nine little green bananas swayin' in de breeze,
They all turn yellow,
An' one a dem sneeze!
Eight little yellow bananas lookin' up to heaven,
One couldn't take de squeeze,
An' dat left seven.
Seven little yellow bananas grabbin' at sticks,
One miss he grip,
An' dat left six.
Six little yellow bananas happy to be alive,
De bird eat another one,

An' den there was five!
Five yellow bananas hear the birds caw,
One fall 'pon de groun',
An' dat left four.
Four yellow bananas now in tree,
One slide off,
Den there was three.
Three yellow bananas gettin' a good view,
One tumble down!
An' dat left two.
Two yellow bananas bright in de sun,
A chile start eatin',
An' dat left only one!

Jamaica

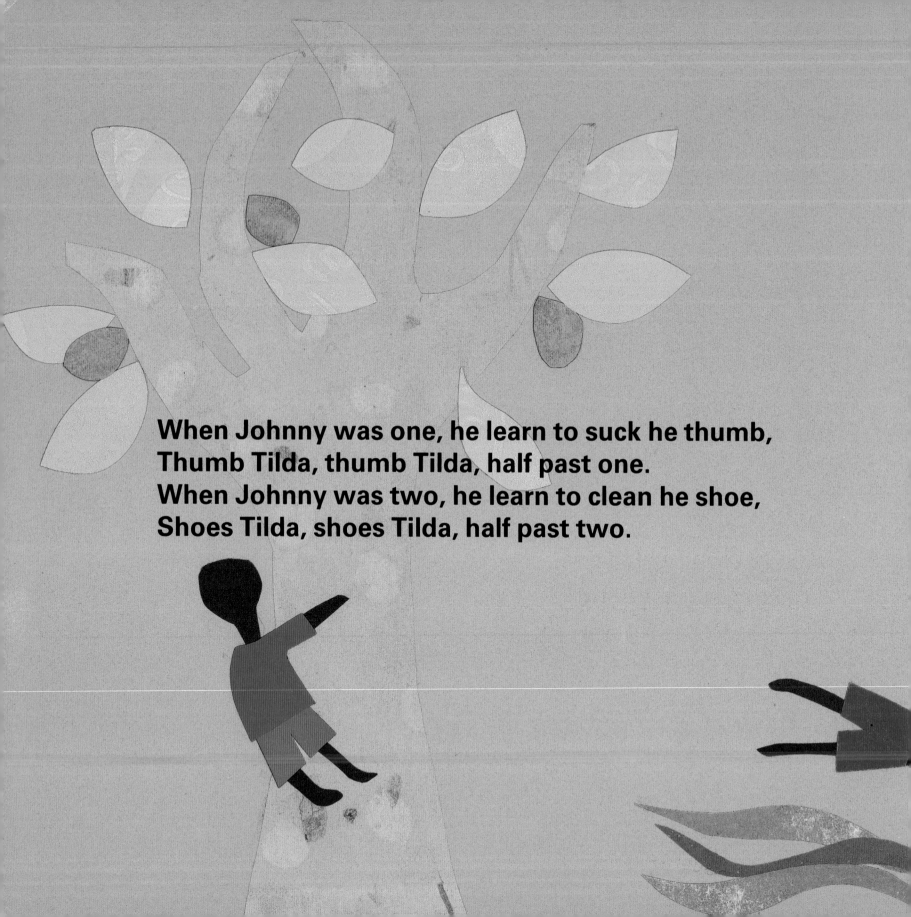

When Johnny was one, he learn to suck he thumb,
Thumb Tilda, thumb Tilda, half past one.
When Johnny was two, he learn to clean he shoe,
Shoes Tilda, shoes Tilda, half past two.

When Johnny was three, he learn to climb mango-tree,
Tree Tilda, tree Tilda, half past three.
When Johnny was four, he learn to shut de door,
Door Tilda, door Tilda, half past four.

When Johnny was five, he learn to dig an' dive,
Dive Tilda, dive Tilda, half past five.
When Johnny was six, he learn to pick up sticks,
Sticks Tilda, sticks Tilda, half past six.

When Johnny was seven, he fly up to heaven,
Heaven Tilda, heaven Tilda, half past seven.
When Johnny was eight, he learn to shut de gate,
Gate Tilda, gate Tilda, half past eight.

When Johnny was nine, he learn to feed de swine,
Swine Tilda, swine Tilda, half past nine.
When Johnny was ten, he learn to feed de hen,
Hen Tilda, hen Tilda, half past ten.

Jamaica

One mongoose fighting a snake.
Two mongoose eating cake.
Three mongoose climbing a tree.
Four mongoose eating cherry.

Dutch West Indies

'Janey, yuh see nobody pass here?'
'No, me friend.'
'Well, one of me dumplins gone.'
'Sarah, yuh see nobody pass here?'
'No, me friend.'
'Well, two of me dumplins gone.'
'Janey, yuh see nobody pass here?'
'No, me friend.'
'Well, three of me dumplins gone.'
'Sarah, yuh see nobody pass here?'
'No, me friend.'
'Well, four of me dumplins gone.'
'Don't tell me so!'
'Four of me dumplins gone.'
'I don't want to know!'
'Four of me dumplins gone.'

Jamaica

Ten rats smell a cat,
De cat snatch one,
De other nine run.
One drown in a river,
De eight start to holler.
One climb a coconut-tree,
Bawlin', 'Yuh can't catch me!'
Seven rats runnin' on a wall,
One slip an' fall.
Six rats rush in a sack,
One stick in a crack
An' sprain he back.

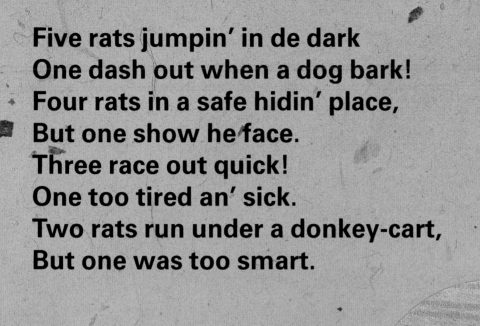

Five rats jumpin' in de dark
One dash out when a dog bark!
Four rats in a safe hidin' place,
But one show he face.
Three race out quick!
One too tired an' sick.
Two rats run under a donkey-cart,
But one was too smart.

Dat leave one
Who didn't want to run,
So de cat catch he,
An' dat's de end of dis furry story.

Virgin Islands

Auntie give me a juicy mango ripin' on de tree,
Uncle give me two orange twice as juicy.
Granny give me three breadfruit,
An' four jack fruit dress-up in prickly suit.
Granpa give me five yam,
I boil dem just like ham.
Cousin Olga gimme six guava,
Tellin' me not to forget her.
An' from de neighbour, Mrs Clare,
I get seven ripe avocado-pear.
De eight bananas in a bunch,
I go eat dem for me lunch!

Tobago

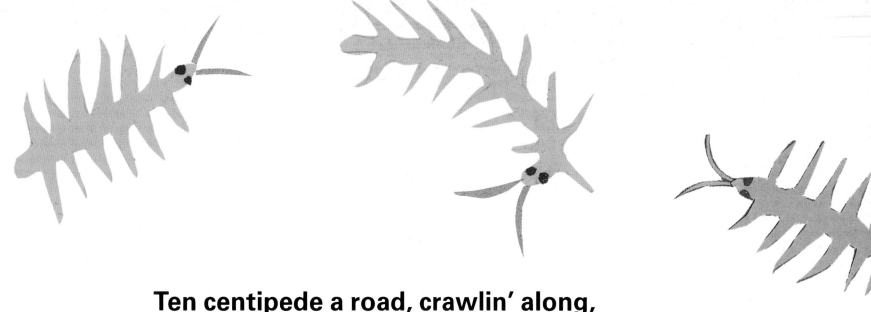

Ten centipede a road, crawlin' along,
Tired pickney chase dem all day long!
Nine centipede a road, beatin' they chest,
Eight centipede a road, siddown takin' rest!
Seven centipede a road, all come last,
Six centipede a road, run so fast!
Five centipede a road, run in de sea,
Four centipede a road, chase dem pickney!
Three centipede a road, big an' thick,
Two centipede a road, run quick,
One centipede a road, lookin' slick!

Jamaica

'pickney' means 'children'

Little girl, skipping fast and slow,
I'll tell you when to go!
From one to ten,
I'll tell you when.
Skip one, skip and jump,
Skip two, fall down with a bump!
Skip three, mind the top drawer,

Skip four, it's smoother on the floor!
Skip five, outdoors in a spin,
Skip six, smash into a bin!
Skip seven, faster! faster! faster!
Skip eight, salt, vinegar, mustard, pepper!
Skip nine, slow down or the rope will break,
Skip ten, that's all I can take.

Martinique

Barefoot Beginners
an imprint of
Barefoot Books
PO Box 95
Kingswood
Bristol
BS30 5BH

Graphic design by Judy Linard, London
Printed and bound in Singapore by Tien Wah Press (Pte) Ltd

This book has been printed on 100% acid-free paper

ISBN 1 901223 86 8

British Cataloguing-in-Publication Data: a catalogue record for this book is available from the British Library

3 5 7 9 8 6 4 2